For my Cowboy, who inspires my dreams, believes I can make them come true, and helps me realize them.

– R.D.

In memory of my parents who were entrepreneurial spirits; with thanks to my co-author Rana DiOrio for the collaborative fun; and with love and gratitude always to Anne, my inspiration and forever partner on the journey.

– E.D.D.

For Jillybean.

– K.M.

ISBN 978-1-939775-12-2

13 12 11 10   1 2 3 4 5 6 7 8 9

Printed in the United States of America

Little Pickle Press, Inc.
3701 Sacramento Street #494
San Francisco, CA 94118
Please visit us at www.littlepicklepress.com.

Library of Congress Control Number: 2015042677
Library of Congress Cataloging-in-Publication Data
Names: DiOrio, Rana, author. | Dryden, Emma D., author.
Title: What Does It Mean To Be An Entrepreneur? | by Rana DiOrio and Emma D. Dryden.
Description: San Francisco: Little Pickle Press, 2016 | Series: What Does It Mean To Be . . .?
Identifiers: LCCN 2015042677 | ISBN 9781939775122
Subjects: LCSH: Entrepreneurship—Juvenile literature. | Businesspeople—Juvenile literature.
Classification: LCC HB615 .D565 2015 | DDC 338/.04—dc23

WHAT DOES IT MEAN TO BE AN ENTREPRENEUR?

By Rana DiOrio & Emma D. Dryden

Illustrated by Ken Min

Little Pickle Press

What does it mean to be an *entrepreneur?*

Does it mean making lots of money? No.

Does it mean
buying a business?
No.

Does it mean
speaking French?
No!

Being an entrepreneur means . . .

... thinking differently
and having original ideas.

. . . following your dream
wholeheartedly and unwaveringly . . .
even if it seems impossible.

. . . saying, "Yes, I can!" when others are saying, "No, you can't."

. . . moving forward although you are afraid.

. . . loving to learn and being curious.

... staying open to surprises.

. . . . taking risks.

... having the humility to learn from your mistakes.

. . . staying positive and excited about the possibilities.

... striving for excellence.

. . . working harder than you ever
imagined—all while feeling great joy.

... feeling confident about exercising your own judgment.

Being an entrepreneur means identifying a need

and being brave and determined enough to create an innovative solution.

So let's encourage each other to discover
if we have what it takes to be an entrepreneur.

And spread the word . . .

If we support entrepreneurs, our world will be even more diverse, interesting, and creative.

Our Mission

Little Pickle Press is dedicated to creating media that fosters kindness in young people—and doing so in a manner congruent with that mission.

Media For A Better World

Little Pickle Press
Environmental Benefits Statement

This book is printed on Appleton Utopia U2:XG Extra Green Paper. It is made with 30% PCRF (Post-Consumer Recovered Fiber) and Green Power. It is FSC®-certified, acid-free, and ECF (Elemental Chlorine-Free). All of the electricity required to manufacture the paper used to print this book is matched with RECS (Renewable Energy Credits) from Green-e® certified energy sources, primarily wind.

Little Pickle Press saved the following resources in green paper, cartons, and boards:

	trees	energy	greenhouse gases	wastewater	solid waste
	Post-consumer recovered fiber displaces wood fiber with savings translated as trees.	PCRF content displaces energy used to process equivalent virgin fiber.	Measured in CO_2 equivalents, PCRF content and Green Power reduce greenhouse gas emissions.	PCRF content eliminates wastewater needed to process an equivalent amount of virgin fiber.	PCRF content eliminates solid waste generated by producing an equivalent amount of virgin fiber through the pulp and paper manufacturing process.
	44 trees	20 mil BTUs	3,793 lbs	20,567 gal	1,377 lbs

Calculations based on research by Environmental Defense Fund and other members of the Paper Task Force and applies to print quantities of 7,500 books.

MIX
Paper from
responsible sources
FSC® C002589
www.fsc.org

Green U Power

PRINTED WITH
SOY INK™

Green-e

PROCESSED CHLORINE FREE

Certified
B
Corporation™
bcorporation.net

B Corporations are a new type of company that use the power of business to solve social and environmental problems. Little Pickle Press is proud to be a Certified B Corporation.

We print and distribute our materials in an environmentally friendly manner,

using recycled paper, soy inks, and green packaging.

About The Authors

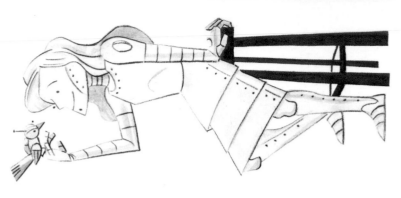

Rana DiOrio

Rana DiOrio has been helping companies grow since graduating from law school. As a lawyer, investor, and investment banker, she has assisted hundreds of management teams in achieving their goals. Becoming a mother inspired Rana to find a way to align her career and values. Her solution was to become an entrepreneur, founding Little Pickle Press in 2009 as a social mission company dedicated to creating media that fosters kindness in children, including her own. Rana sits on the Executive Committee and Board of the Independent Book Publishers Association, and the Advisory Boards of GrapeSeed, Stepping Stories, and Vanderbilt University School of Law. Her personal pursuits include fitness training, practicing yoga, reading non-fiction and children's books, dreaming big dreams and helping other entrepreneurs realize theirs, and, of course, being global, green, present, safe, and kind. She lives in San Francisco, California with The Cowboy and her three Little Pickles. Follow Rana DiOrio on Twitter at @ranadiorio.

Emma D. Dryden

Emma D. Dryden lives in the home in which she grew up in New York City, where she was raised by entrepreneurs. Her father was a self-employed actor and her mother a self-employed writer/researcher. A longtime children's book editor and publisher, Emma spent over twenty years working at a large publishing company before starting her own children's book editorial and publishing consultancy firm, drydenbks LLC, in 2010. Books Emma has edited have won numerous awards, she's an Advisory Board member of the Society of Children's Book Writers & Illustrators, and she speaks extensively on the art and craft of writing for children. Her blog, "Our Stories, Ourselves", explores the connections between the human experience and the writing experience. *What Does It Mean To Be An Entrepreneur?* is her debut picture book. Visit Emma at www.drydenbks.com.

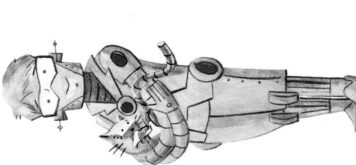

About The Illustrator

Ken Min

Ken grew up on the works of Margret & H.A. Rey, William Joyce, and DC Comics. He was born and raised in Los Angeles and studied illustration at Art Center, College of Design. He has storyboarded for various commercials and animated TV shows such as The PJs, Futurama, and The Fairly OddParents. His illustration work has been recognized numerous times by the Society of Children's Book Writers & Illustrators (SCBWI). In 2012, the first picture book he illustrated, *Hot, Hot Roti For Dada-Ji*, received the Picture Book Honor Award for Literature from the Asian Pacific American Librarians Association (APALA).

These days, you will find Ken illustrating, storyboarding, writing, and dreaming up stories for children.

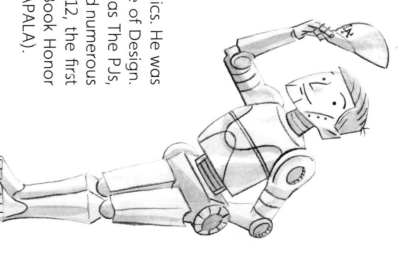